Poems

from

The Big Table

Jeff —
Enjoyed our talk
by the bar & glad
to see you again.
Good times on the
mountain. Graeme

Churn Dash Press

Acknowledgments

Jerri Beck: "Girls Grow Up Knowing His Name" first appeared in *Baker's Dozen* and "A Need to Know Basis" first appeared in *Birmingham Arts Journal.*

Robert Boliek: "Dogfish," "To a Sunflower" and "As Time Goes By" first appeared in *The Formalist*; "Fledglings" and "Plato Has a Bad Dream" first appeared in *Romantics Quarterly*, while "The Muse of Thermodynamics Speaks Her Mind," "In the Museum of Natural History," "A Snapshot from Chichén-Itzá," "Langley," "Doctor Jung Dreams of a Confrontation with the Alchemist Paracelsus, Who Says," "A Scrap of Ancient History," and "The Passionate Shepherd's Response to the Nymph" first appeared in *Birmingham Arts Journal, Troubadour, Edge City Review, Hellas, Legal Studies Forum, Mobius,* and *RE:AL*, respectively.

Suzanne Coker: "Taking the Veil" and "Look at Me" first appeared in *Birmingham Arts Journal.*

Irene Latham: "Peeling an Orange" first appeared in *SouthLit* and "Muir Woods" first appeared in *Birmingham Arts Journal.*

Manufactured in Birmingham, Alabama

Library of Congress Cataloging-in-Publication Data

Beck, Jerri, editor
    Poems from the Big Table

ISBN: 0-9791112-0-X

2006938548

Churn Dash Press
P.O. Box 660099
Birmingham, AL 35266-0099

Contents

Big Table Poets

At Thanksgiving, reunions, and other family celebrations, children are usually relegated to the kids' tables, while adults feast at the "big table." Writers, too, spend a lot of time at the flimsy card tables and wobbly TV trays that often constitute kids' tables. But at some point, if they are lucky, survival and experience qualify them for the BIG TABLE. Since 2002, the Big Table Poets have literally met at a large table at a Birmingham bookstore. The group has organized performances and now ventures into publication. Membership is by invitation. While this book includes work by only the five original members, future publications will include newer members. With this volume, we welcome you to *our* big table.

JERRI BECK

tribal markings

when i was a child
on the reservation
a missionary told me
of african tribes
that cut
the faces of children
packing the wounds
with manure
to insure scarring
branding for recognition

with edges sharper
than primitive knives
i was branded
filled with infections
harsher than
the dung of cattle

but
like the tattooed sailor
i have come
to love my scars
sometimes
at night
i touch them
hard
and stony
in soft flesh

Night/Fall

Outside, the oaks protest.
The wind plays the night
in a minor key. The street,
so far away, empties
as the city's quiet roar
drives home in falling snow.

Night, the magician, shrinks
this room to a closet. Light
narrows to a splinter, disappears
as if an iron door closed
across the eastern sky.

The fire draws shadows
on the darkened floor;
the cat ghostwalks
to the fading flame,
curls into a gray note
on the hearth. Even she
was not prepared to see you.

The two years gone
knock heavy on the walls.
We do not name the war
and yet it moves
across your face, against
my chest fighting
to breathe.
And when you speak,
your mouth
gives voice to snow.

Homestead

I live in a corner
behind a chair
that grows larger
in the dark.
The walls
looming above me
shudder in expansion
like an iceberg
swelling.

My stomach wraps
its tight fist
around a stone
there from birth.

My locked knees
have grown rigid.
The ankles, frozen,
have not moved
since the sun ran away.

At night
I can feel rats,
in the hollow walls,
moving against my feet.
I wonder if they have names
for their children
caught in our traps.

I live in this corner—
feet pressing one silent wall;
back braced against its cornermate.
Some days the light finds me here,
hypotenused to the right angles
of a house no longer
small enough for two.

Lessons

When I was five in North Carolina
I knew about Wilbur and Orville
and the secrets of flight, and
I wanted to fly. Completely
understanding aerodynamics, I
rode my tricycle around my
grandmother's porch, pumping
the pedals so hard my knees rose
to the height of my chin,
and I went faster with every
circle, feeling the wind roar
through my hair. And when
I knew I was approaching the
speed of light, I steered the tri
cycle off the porch and into
welcoming air.

Girls Grow Up Knowing His Name

Our mothers warned us about him,
singled him out in news accounts
and whispered cautions of the night.
We learned to travel
in pairs and listen for footsteps,
to lock the doors and never
talk to strangers.

In Daytona, tanned and smiling
at the corner of Main Street,
he asked directions
I didn't know.
In Miami he was tall
and bearded, walking attack
dogs around the fence
that marked his borders.

I didn't see him when I loaded the car,
but he was there.
His eyes trapped mine
in the rear-view mirror
on the empty interstate to Arkansas.
My left arm was sunburned
when I stopped in Fort Smith.
He offered lotion
and pumped the gas
slower than usual.

I gave his name to every face,
memorized the angle of his body
leaning against old buildings.
I've seen him all my life—
there and there and there and
here
where he didn't know
he would be tonight,
where the roads tangle and weave
before moving in separate directions.

I have seen him start as if to move
then pull back.
But he was always there
just beyond the doors and windows
closed against the dark.

Last night in the laundromat,
I heard his footsteps at my back.
Running to lock a door or find
a place to hide, I saw
deserted street, my empty car,
my tightened face coming back at me
from windows, windshield, gleaming
chrome of washing machines.

From far away, I heard men laugh
as they left the only bar in town.
And all around, my face stared at itself
growing whiter in the night.

A Need to Know Basis

What do I need to know
that I knew before
he cut my head open,
rerouted the veins
and stapled me shut?

Have I forgotten a name
I once called out
in my sleep?
Or the touch I used
to calm the cat?
Or the color of the room
I grew up in?

Where did everything go
that wasn't left
that early winter morning
when a doctor
saved my life
but not my memory.

Bi•Polar

For the past two weeks,
each electrical thing
has mutinied, rebelled, just plain
gone to hell—
been a magnetic jolt
forced through water and land
in a charged sleight of hand.

And each death has been mine:
like being filleted
with a dull rusting blade
or trying to grow gills
so my lungs can be filled
with air where none lives.

Buying a million new shirts
would not be enough
to fill the broad gulf;
a black hole so dense
it has long since
sucked inside.

Eve

I'm tired of carrying the weight
of the Fall. What a stupid thing
to say. As if one woman
changed history. God only knows
who they would have blamed
if I hadn't been there.

The serpent? Sure, like I talked
to some snake. This is exactly
the kind of thing a man would say.

Do you think it was easy
living with a perfect man?
He wasn't perfect, you know.
He was missing a rib.

I tell you now, I don't apologize
for anything I ever did.
If paradise had been enough,
there would have been no need
for a taste of something more.

ROBERT BOLIEK

The Muse of Thermodynamics Speaks Her Mind

That poor man Keats was wrong: Timelessness
is not pretty. I know—I can stop Time.
I've even done it once or twice, for kicks:
It's always the same and O so sad—each hapless
spider is welded to its web of cable,
while roses tumesce on iron stems, red-faced
in static gardens. (Even the bumblebees
are stalled, ridiculously fat, above
the stone tulips.) White clouds cling to the sun
like big dead rats at a poisoned orange,
and where before the people danced: *Imagine!*—
The world is cluttered with countless wooden dolls.

A Snapshot from Chichén-Itzá

My eye is like this camera's lens—
Unblinking at the Terribles—
As I focus on my wife who grins
Beside the Mayan Rack of Skulls.

Is it so strange that we should play
Where they once beat a sacred drum?
The gods they feared have had their day,
And we are certain spring will come.

To a Sunflower

The maker and breaker of worlds, did He
Linger longer, that third full day,
Indulging some florid fantasy
Creating thee? Or was it, say,
A spur of the moment kind of thing,
An afterthought, a jab of the brush
Against the canvas, an instant's fling
In the fury of that six-day rush?
For the sport among flowers are you,
My striving, gaudy, gaunt *princesse*—
Beautiful? No, but this is true:
None can challenge your wild excess.
And so I wonder, do I see
In you the Plan? An accident?
Delightful serendipity
Or the glory of the firmament?

Dogfish

I propose that English poetry and biology should be
taught as usual, but that at irregular intervals poetry
students should find dogfishes on their desks and
biology students should find Shakespeare sonnets
on their dissecting boards.

—Walker Percy

Expecting the marriage of true minds, I find
Instead this rough-skinned, finny fish, slate-gray
On top and white below, dorsally-spined,
And purportedly of the family *Squalidae.*
I hold the knife but do not think of death:
Rolling through waters light as air, with skies
Of silver above, the ocean floor beneath,
Serenely submarine my dogfish flies
Through the mid-Atlantic suburbs of its youth.
I pause before the image fades. The sleek
Body conceals, but Percy knew the truth:
To hope to find, one first must choose to seek.
       So he used the knife without regret or grief—
       Dissecting the anatomy of unbelief.

In the Museum of Natural History

Scientists Say . . . Fossils Prove Dinosaur-to-Bird Link
—Headline from the *New York Times*

Skyward to a vaulted ceiling
Extend the fossil's curving bones;
A younger me, wide-eyed with feeling,
Could animate those lifeless stones:

I'd conjure up a covering flesh
Suitable for lines reptilian,
A scaly skin (appropriate dress!),
And flashing eyes of bright vermillion;

I'd watch the beast regain lost grace
As subtle former muscles flexed
And count the teeth in the fearsome face
Of dread *Tyrannosaurus rex.*

Whatever I imagined though
About this robust mass of chalk
Was just a small boy's puppet show
Compared to scientific talk:

How Darwin's *Beagle* on her quest
Around the Cape and further still
Sailed far beyond a human past,
Five billion years before the Fall;

How brittle scales could once conspire
To feather unrestricted sky—
The lizard brave the changeling's fire
And like the risen phoenix fly.

I tell myself I'm happier here
Beneath this harsh relentless light:
"I'm a grown-up now," I think and stare
And strain to see the bones take flight.

Fledglings

I climbed our prison tower's winding stair,
Unfolded wings of feather, twine, and wax,
Tied them to Icarus with cords of flax,
And then I said, "Beware the upper air."

He never heard. He soared without a care
Into the hot eye of the sun, the wax
Slowing melting.
                Then, he was gone.
                              And the backs
Of the waves sported feathers everywhere.

Fathers, which of you will escape the fear
I knew that day?
                You'll buy her skates when she
Turns three, fasten them with exceeding care,
Give warnings she will not or cannot hear,
A first reluctant push as she rolls free—
And then you'll look down helpless from the middle air.

As Time Goes By

In the movie *Casablanca,* Ilsa and Rick
will always have Paris, always. Bogart-Blaine
may drink his bourbon straight and feel no pain,
but in the final reel (his neatest trick)
he'll always set young Ilsa free: he'll pick
the hero's life and put her on the plane.
Let the years roll by, his image will remain:
Rick Blaine is free from Time's arithmetic.

Indeed, with film one seems to watch the man
grow young as one grows old. Though Highest Art
has always sought this dream of timelessness,
should it not pity the aging movie fan?

As time goes by, the scenes he knows by heart
will mock lost youth—when a kiss was still a kiss.

Plato Has a Bad Dream

Socrates professes to know nothing; we naturally
treat this as irony, but it could be taken seriously.

—Betrand Russell

"Do you know anything you think you know?"
asked Socrates, come back from the dead. "The wise,"
he said, "confess their ignorance, despise
the mob of easy truths and yearn to go
to the sources—the sky above, the earth below,
the circle of birth and death. With opened eyes,
they bow or kneel before these mysteries
but know they do not, will not, can not know.
Chained in a five-walled cell of sense, our thought-
bedeviled minds seek light outside the cell,
but find no light amenable to sight;
in fact, our vision is a wall. Had I taught
you well you'd see the world is one dark hell—
a cave, where shadows dance into the night."

Langley

American astronomer and pioneer in the design
and construction of airplanes . . . . He invented
the bolometer, used to determine the intensity
of solar radiation.
—Funk & Wagnalls New Encyclopedia

The bicycle brothers were not alone: he too
had dreams heavier than air, envied the birds,
grew crow's feet staring squint-eyed at that blue,
unbroken sky. (Maybe he dreamed of the words
they'd write the day that Langley mastered flight.)

Then the bad news came (dateline: Outer Banks)—
how two Ohio boys had done all right,
had gotten it to fly, the glory, and the thanks.

So Samuel Pierpont Langley, who once had caught
evanescing sunbeams in a magic jar,
became a footnote overnight—a naught—
despite his dreaming well and going far.

May I reserve this space for those who place—
For the Langleys who make a race a race?

Doctor Jung Dreams of a Confrontation with the Alchemist Paracelsus, Who Says

Is the phoenix crowned with a gold mandala?
The circle closed at last? Can you ennoble
A leaden egg with a yolk of gold, or trouble
The water *(the aqua regia)* with the breath of Allah?

Other deities will do: My Cabala
Embraces lots of gods on a scale quite global
(But mostly desert types from Egypt's rubble)
Transplanted to our northern soil. Follow?

So tell me—is the phoenix crowned with a gold
Mandala? Can you ennoble the egg of the soul
With glimmerings of perfect gold—that flash
Of nascent genius—as the ancient sages hold?

If not, consider this as makes one whole:
To free the soul, reduce ego to ash.

A Scrap of Ancient History

In the camp of Alexander,
Blacksmiths tinkered,
Ministers whispered,
And Captains lingered.

An unburned salamander
Was rescued from the embers
And then precisely quartered
By the hierophants who mattered.

"The world will somehow prosper"
Was their solemn verdict rendered
(As if the entrails of a lizard
Could tie continents together).

But the late lord king and master
(O mighty Alexander!)—
Embracing his one thousand gods—
Cared no further for the future.

The Passionate Shepherd's Response to the Nymph

Let rivers rage to choking dust
And birds go silent if they must—
Do you expect to turn this page
In the twilight of that distant age?

My simple gifts of leaf and flower
Were only meant to last an hour:
If soon withered and forgotten,
They are in Time, not Reason, rotten.

For while you brood upon your rock,
Four horsemen watch a ticking clock,
And all we are and have will pass
The way of summer rains and grass.

I ask you when (with honey tongue!)
I spoke the words "forever young"
Or claimed an ageless, deathless youth
Or more of life than this sharp truth:

If human love like human life
Is hurried, desperate, all too brief,
What greater gift is mine to give
Than my brief love, while I still live?

So live with me and be my love
For your replies my pleasures prove
As surely as the rocks grow cold
Or Time drives flocks from field to fold.

SUZANNE COKER

In the Cavern

To my right and far, far above
is the hardest white ever seen,
tiny diamond light, not twinkling,
pressed from this coal dark, onyx
seamed with grief, scarred
by conquerors and gunshot.

The tour guide intones *only*
at the bottom of the sea is there
darkness so complete

and I just grin
where no one can see me.

The Angel

of near-death
watches a lot of tv, has asthma,
allergies, and irritated skin.
She posts tentative warnings:
bridge may ice in cold weather, smoking
may be hazardous to your health,
goes to lots of twelve-step meetings,
adds drama to the leads.

She blesses the tantrums of very young women
and has an awful crush on Death—
that black hood, the scythe, so decisive!
She flirts with him shamelessly, speeds
through blind country crossroads at full dark,
steering with one pinky, holding
a jug of hot coffee while her other hand
cranks the radio. She takes up extreme sports,
dangles over broken edges, swims with sharks.

She goes wherever she thinks Death will be,
sits at the bedsides of hypochondriacs, but
when he shows up she can't look at him,
slinks away to a bright-light-and-tunnel show
calls up her friends to whimper
about the torments of near-love.

Haunted

Ahead are men in masks
and women who shriek like ghouls.

Soon we will buy tickets,
but for now, out here in line
the air is clear

and a girl about sixteen dances
around her boyfriend, grins,
sasses, punches his arm,

flies up and down the thick parade
of fool's wisdom, showing off
her freedom from what anyone thinks.

Crazy, he headshakes, proud
to possess her, to claim her dragon jacket
and flowing hair.

Recaptured, she plants
boots in the gravel and sags
into him, chest to chest,

her eyes blaze unmet past
his shoulder, fresh despair
demanding *is this my year? is it?*

Out of Line

This glimpse turns the world to a bruise,
a child dragged by hands
that terrify her because
they are her father's.

She had grabbed for candy
it's true, wanted
to show mommy

not Daddy. How he hit
first, no hesitation, the red rising
behind his two days of beard,
how he pulled her arm
and bent to her, whispered
god knows what straight
into her ear, shame
collapsing her little strength,
screams gone to whimpers
as he led her away

her mother added two boxes
of candy to the checkout,
hesitated, then piled up
two of every candy from the rack
and asked for a separate ticket.

She would not
meet the cashier's eyes,
and I would not meet hers.

Taking the Veil

My mother's veil was heavy, dark, and fell
not in front of her eyes, but behind them.
Not always a veil, it began
as a limber shadow that danced
with her, urged her to dive
off the yacht and swim down
the moon's path on Lake Pontchartrain.

The shower in her New York apartment
shot water from all directions.
Her father called her a flying waitress,
her roommate was never there.
She lived on leftovers, it took months
to save money for a flimsy stoplight dress.

Sometime after marriage, the shadow
became insistent. It stood
wherever she did, hard as a door
she would have to open or shut.
She tried to stave it off with babies,
but the shadow ate them,

leaving only their squalling. Finally
she stepped into the silhouette,
allowed herself numb
grace, went through motions
in a pale gray dress, found recipes
to explain her grasp of wine.

Look At Me

The red dress turned
a bridegroom from
his bride, temporarily.

The red dress caught
a soldier, let his hands
past its buttons on
a bench by the river.

The red dress needed
dry cleaning, got
dunked in the sink instead,

shriveled and clung,
buttons chipped,
hem puckered.

The shoes that matched
cracked at the heels,
trying to click home.

Read It Again

The book breaks, dried
by ten years on the shelf.
Its words sing more now
of the worth of editors
than the dazzle of creation.
Themes emerge like lemon ink
cooked on a brighter bulb.

An old bookmark on page 205, his name,
our last address printed on a ticket from a bank
that's been bought out. I pressed this lesson on him
and he took notes: page 139, middle. Page 184.

Diverted from story to history, I look for patterns
which refuse to be clues. *The Wounded Land* remains
a closed world, scaling into dust, covers fallen,
our loss become a lifetime without maps.

New light leads me to my mark. I read
to the end of the chapter, retrace the story,
use packing tape to mend the spine.

Translation

You never know who will survive
a shipwreck. I thought I would
die of salt water, then sun,
then emptiness, forgetting
all I knew on the mainland.
Speech is something I invented
to teach the gulls.

At first I mistook you for seaweed,
then you groaned. Your eyes
the color of the lagoon
in a storm, your skin raw,
the thinnest glint of gold
around your neck. I think
you said *who are you* and
I said *toli kai, ka liki,* meaning
get up, are you all right?

You thought it was my name.
I didn't mind. I was busy
deciding how to forage for two,
whether your leg would heal itself,
where to bury you if not.

Now I can tell when you've walked
past my hut, your prints are larger
than mine, one foot turned outward.
I know you expect to find a tribe.
I try to invent words to tell you
we are the only natives here.

Head

The John Wayne head
began as a mannequin
innocently beheaded,
filmed, then ignored
until Wonkafest,
where it gained
a fluorescent target
painted around one eye
and a purple splat
of lipstick.

It may at one time have
worn a crown of thorns, or
of Christmas lights. Then
it was casually encased
in a plastic Reagan mask,
eventually pasted over
with a photocopied Wayne.

For a while, the Dutch Duke
modeled fright wigs, but when
did it become so lifelike,
absorb all layers?

He doesn't know, but can recall
the exact moment she
made him stow it in the garage.

Jack and Diane

Peaches come from a can.
            —The Presidents of the United States of America

Teacher, where do songs come from?

I'm glad you asked. There
is a Music Factory, located
at the foot of the Background Mountains.

It's a wonderful place, where
young girls are given piercings
and collagen injections and taught
to dance, where young men get
many tattoos and sometimes
drug habits. They also learn
to dance, because as everyone
knows, you can't sell a song
without dancing.

Oh, says the little girl, drops her eyes
to her folded hands. Oh, says
the little boy, shuffles his clumsy feet.

After school they run out
to the nameless woods.
She shakes a tin can
full of bottle caps. He
strums a broken old
guitar. They laugh,
and move their hips. But

it isn't Music.

Guerrilla Poetry

The tactics of art are not kind, no time
for prisoners and nothing to feed them.
Hostages will only slow us down

as we sweep through the last village
on Inspiration Plain, five minutes
before national troops arrive.

We call the horses, gather muskets
and swords, set a few volunteers
for decoy, a dust trail leading in circles.

There are pens in the bandoliers worn
crossed on our chests. We hide in the woods,
watching for loyalists. As we starve

in our camp behind the darkened hills
we sing of beautiful fate. Traitors
and the wounded are killed at dawn.

We are not above accepting foreign aid.
The Cause despoils only those who wish it,
and stories are the mines we leave,
our violent mystery.

IRENE LATHAM

Muir Woods

Here we begin
again,

where redwoods
rise on all sides

as if born
whole

and placed
by some god

whose one decree
was silence.

The seed
cannot know

its own greatness,
and we can

only hold hands,
take pictures

that tell nothing
of all we hope for

or where we've been,
or where we'll be

when the seed
is no longer a seed

but a giant
with foot-thick skin,

its arms
reaching toward

an ocean
it will never see.

Peace Time: Riyadh, Saudi Arabia, 1975

The walls were purple
except at night when they turned
black as roses withered on the vine,

bare bulb in the hallway
blazing a path to the bathroom
but the little girl would not

brave the army of roaches skittering
across the wood floor and up the walls,
Sendak's Wild Things come to life,
but where was Max, their King?

Alone in her room, the little girl
listened for the tap of her father's feet
climbing the steep stairs
but heard only the rumble
of his voice from the belly of the house

while outside the tiny window
curtained with purple pleated dotted-Swiss
goats bleated from atop cars parked in the alley
Go Away, Go Away

but the little girl could not go
because of the roaches
and because of the high wall hiding the house,

the iron gate guarded by men with brambled beards,
baby brother asleep in Mother's bed
his hair glistening red as the dunes of An Nafud,

grandmother's quilt sent all the way from the States,
thick
but not thick enough
to stop the war unfolding in her room

the tickle of tiny legs,
the trickle between her thighs,
the sticky-wet deaths no one ever sees.

Creed

I believe if you follow
the wall far enough
you will eventually find a door
that no god is going to open for you—
just you with your gnarled fingers
curling around the knob.

I believe in dirt under fingernails,
do-it-yourself, mud puddles,
the smell of fresh-cut grass.

I believe in serendipity,
coincidence, random
accidents that defy explanation
because there is no explaining pain
or the lack of it.

I believe whatever is, *is;*
"meant to be" is a fig growing
on an imaginary tree.

I believe Adam and Eve still
inhabit our gardens, whisper
to serpents and savor apples,
make wild love one minute,
drop their eyes and cover
themselves the next.

I believe in cliffs that become canyons,
canyons that cradle rivers,
rivers that leave
and keep on leaving
every day there's earth, air, sky.

I believe the ocean is the womb
where we begin and end,
the shore with its grit and shards of shell
the battlefield where we fight
our most natural impulses,
our tongues parched, our skin blistered

and raw, our voices crying
to be heard and understood,
for someone, anyone, to
save me, goddammit, I'm drowning here.

I believe the wind carries
our secrets like seeds,
plants them on deserted islands
where they grow into trees with coconuts,
sweet milk waiting for the washed-up,
the down-on-their-luck, the ones
whose cups are empty
but who somehow find
the strength to climb.

I believe there is nothing more real
than love you can't see,
nothing more powerful than our minds
surging in dream,
our sleeping legs pumping like pistons
until almost, almost…
then waking in a bed with the one
you love more than anything,
aching to touch him
but not touching him
because there is such sweet
torture in waiting.

I believe in dust to dust
and grey skies and choices
that are neither right nor wrong.

I believe forgiveness is the best way
to lighten a load, yet without the yoke
one never learns all he is capable of.

I believe *everything will be okay,*
and even when it's not
if you follow the wall far enough,
you will find a door.

Peeling an Orange

After years of no words
you came for the weekend,
prodigal father spotted now
by sun and age, hair a beach
of white sand, bare in places.

This is what's real, you said,
when it was time for you to leave.
Not meaning we should forget the past,
just, this is what's important now.

I reached for your hand
across the oak table with its
nicks and scratches, our shared
history and separate ones etched
in each knot and blemish.

This is what's real:
I pulled your car around so that you
might avoid the flight of stairs,
watched your knee nearly
give way on the one front step.
Carried your bag, tucked it in
the trunk, gave you a kiss.

You waved, then I watched
your car disappear below the hill,
street empty, birds silent.
Went inside and peeled an orange.
Let the pieces drop to that place
where our hands had been.
Savored the sweetness.

And There Was An Orange Moon

Last night I waited six hours
for the sound of your key in the door
my body curled in a tight ball
and I thought, this is what it's like
to know you'll soon be born,
here in this white-sheeted world
its walls rising and falling
with each fluttering breath

and you driving toward me
down highways made unfamiliar
by darkness and time
then out of nowhere
(you told me this morning)
moon like a pumpkin
your hand turning the knob,
heart thrumming in its iron cage.

Upon Hearing the News
That Pluto is No Longer a Planet

Turns out
size really does matter.

Pluto's too small,
our children are too fat.

Would the terrorists
have targeted a smaller building?

Would McDonald's sell so many fries
if they weren't supersized?

Nothing is certain.
Death? Taxes?

Sure, one could argue.
I say, there is only love.

And call it a dwarf
or call it a genuine planet

Pluto's still there,
relentless in its orbit,

the sun shines on though we're told
it might not eventually

and I still give every star your name,
however fleeting.

First Day of School

Sixteen six-year-olds
sit tall in their desks,
their faces shining
like a brand-new box
of sharp, unbroken crayons.

How long before the teacher
in all her goodness and wisdom
asks them to pull out their rulers,
erase, create rows of paper dolls?

I suppose it must be done—
there are lines to stand in,
inside voices to maintain
and hands that must not touch
from here on out.

But I ask you, Dear Teacher:
what do I say to my son
who has never been able
to color inside the lines?
How do I explain
his sun is not wrong just because
you want it to be yellow,

how can I teach him
                           to find
the beauty
              of a random afternoon
        thunderstorm that paints
    the world
                    black,
the brilliance
        of a sky
                   that can't be
                              contained

when you keep telling him
stop, no, not like that?

At the Hardware Store

A blonde in blue-jeans stands behind the counter—
she doesn't know socket-wrench from flat-head driver

but her smile spreads easy as strawberry jam
and her fingers glide over the register

like pond-skaters under a mid-summer moon.
Need a half-pound of Nichol's screw-grip nails,

I say, and she furrows her brow then brightens,
blush staining the constellation of freckles

on her chest and I never wanted to be
a freckle so much in my fifty-year life

then that smile again like a flash of lightning
on a black-cloud day, and I suck in my gut,

smile right back, not sure what I'll do with those nails
but ready to erect a steel skyscraper

and empty my accounts, if that's what it takes.

Black Dress

—for my mother

Where is the black dress
I watched you cut
from satin sheets?

Handmade with love
the label declared,
as they all did.

What did I know then of love?

I thought I needed
to rid myself of you
to become me

so I put your creations in bags,
left them at the curb
for a truck to carry away.

Now your joints swell,
your sewing machine stays covered,
and I have money for dresses.

But I want them back,
those dresses that were born
of your mind and fingers

the black dress
out of style now
but classic

the way black dresses are,
the way we learn about love
too late.

If Not for Starlings

We walk the trail
shaded by oak and cypress

watch as the combined
weight of a hundred birds

splits a common cedar
the way a knife sinks

into a loaf of bread,
bending but not breaking.

You've got to admire
their decisiveness,

the way the starlings lift
and turn,

choose again
the cedar,

its strength and flexibility
a certainty to them,

unknown to us
until this moment.

BARRY MARKS

Upgrade

- NW 1195, Boston to Atlanta

Because he was too slow
on the eTicket machine,
poor Ken couldn't upgrade to First Class as I did.
He's back there with the po' folks,
the ones who are traveling to see newborn grandkids,
or Key West for the first time, while I
glide effortlessly through the clouds,
the airways greased with a complimentary Bloody Mary,
a Captain of Industry in Seat 5-D.

I look about the cabin for the sneak-thief
who got Ken's seat.
Is it the fat, bald burgher in 2-A
drinking his second pre-lunch Scotch
even before we lift off? Is it
the chicken-necked woman in 2-B
nervously reading the emergency card?

Is it one of the Golf Guys in 3-A or B
sharing a chuckle over the putts they missed yesterday
or something about Debi, who dots the "i"
with a plump, expectant heart,
danced on their table last night
and told them she's a grad student at B.U.?
I bet they believed that,
just as they bought the serious eye contact
telling them they were special.

Or maybe it's Renata in 5-C, whose elbow
is touching mine
as she continues to talk on her cell phone
even though the doors are shut
about her trip from Boston to Hong Kong,
paid for by her travel agency as a perk and, no doubt,
a reward for exemplary service.

I am, God help me, forced to eavesdrop on her while
she does irreparable damage to the plane's
navigation system with her cell signal,
interrupting vectors and ground speed algorithms,
putting our lives at risk
        with something Cindy
        just has to hear
        about Cat Cay
        this time of year.
I wonder if the Golf Guys would find her attractive?

As soon as the 767 lifts off, I will
order another free Bloody Mary. How nice
to have a drink named after you,
even if it memorializes mass murder.
How nice to fly free to Hong Kong and
advise your friends on world travel issues.

How nice to upgrade to First Class
for only $50 or some Frequent Flyer Miles.
How nice to believe, at that level
men reserve for such things,
that you have paid $140
for nude dances to a woman who yearns
to run off with you
for a weekend of guilt-free sex
and only you, only you.

Coyote . . .

or maybe a fox, he had no business
in the woods between our deck and
our neighbor's new swimming pool,
but there he was, trotting off
like he was surveying his backyard,
tail swaggering between the brambles.

What if he is the advance scout
for a war party, the dispossessed
risen to reclaim their birthright?
He will return with others of his kind
and bear, boar, bison
bent on driving us back to the city.

They will attack just before dawn,
led, no doubt, by a reconnaissance squad
of bats squeaking the coordinates.
The attackers will set up perimeters
(squirrels should make superb sentries)
and a mobile HQ atop the water tower.
A gaggle of geese will provide air cover,
sacrificing themselves into F-16 intakes and
Apache blades when the National Guard counterattacks.

Perhaps they will enlist allies
among the insect world: roaches, flies
and spiders putting off their internecine conflict
to unite against the poisoning, heavy-footed foe;
or worse, they will send emissaries
to the ghost-shirted assassins,
microbes, bacilli and fungi,
the mutating viral horde,
to sweep off their reservations
and attack with lethal bio-weaponry.

Olde Weatherly will fall to the insurrectionists,
then New Weatherly and the nameless
office park across the street.
They will reclaim 665 Weatherly Lane.
Vines will violate our precious possessions,
choking Beanie Babies and Barbies,
evicting Monet prints from our walls.

A family of armadillos will nest
in the master bath,
while deer doze in our bed
as a solitary 'possum
sways in my hammock.

The occupying force
will forage the pantry,
Shermanizing,
animal bummers loaded down
with Fritos and Fruit Roll-ups
scurrying into the wild night.

They will eat my daughter's loyalist dog;
I assume the cats
will quickly turn coat.

As a final indignity, some furry lockpick
will free our parakeets
to soar out the shattered bay window
into the spring air, their wings
stretched in unfettered glory,
celebrating the joy
of the undomesticated sun.

Aftermath

When you told me to get out, your anger
punched a hole through our marriage;
a black spot hung in the air
in the kitchen, in between us.

When I looked to you, it obscured your face,
so I tried walking to the side, but it was still there,
a black spot as big as your fist.

It made a sucking sound
and began to grow.

My first thought was to find something
to plug it up, yours, to your credit,
was for the children, who you loaded into the car
and drove off, leaving me with the blackness
as it swelled into the dining room.

I ran upstairs for a Bible
but when I turned around
it was advancing up the steps and
it backed me into the bedroom,
into the closet, into a corner and
all I could see was black so I knew
it was on me and I closed my eyes
and held my breath but I had to
breathe so I inhaled and when
I opened my eyes the lights were on
and everything was back the way it should be.

At least that's what I thought,
damn you,
until I looked in the mirror.

Teaching the Angels to Dance

The wings, that is the worst problem.
Their wings scrape the carpet and trip
cherubim and seraphim alike until

with a snort that somehow
hangs musical in the air,
they shoot to the ceiling for a breather.

"Listen to the beat," I plead, but
drum and bass seem to pass through them,
they are lost in melody.
Michael closes his eyes and
unconsciously takes off;
he bumps his head on the chandelier
and settles back to the floor,
blushing, shrugging an apology.

Raphael stumbles into the china cabinet,
Tzaphkiel and Tzadkiel collide,
Metatron practically somersaults over the sofa,
none of them able to translate their innate grace,
their light-drenched, aerodynamic beauty
into the simplest of steps.
I joke that perhaps I should find them a pin,
but that falls flat before empty, beatific smiles.

Only Death seems to get it right,
the perfect partner, following my lead,
her dark eyes glowing,
her balance flawless as
she twirls and spins so light on her feet
she makes me feel like Fred Astaire

until Gabriel cuts in
with a whisper that this is one dance
I should probably sit out.

Daughter

The monster under your bed
is named Bobby or Chris.
He parked his Camaro down the block.

The witch with the gingerbread house
is teaching you not to eat,
or perhaps to puke on command.
You have come to think of secrecy as the art of survival,
the way to live happier ever after, which explains
why you lied about calling me last night
and everything else.

I know that you and Bobby/Chris
will probably sneak out later
on the Harley your mother bought you
and ride into the blood-red sunset,
where the clouds heroically smash into the sky.
You think this is the way dreams
and people die and come true.

When you were born, I didn't care if
you were boy or girl, blonde or red-topped,
as long as you had "10 of each" and your organs
were in the proper configuration.
When you started school, I didn't look for
A's so long as you came home each day
and woke up the next morning.

Now, ADD worries me, but not at all
compared with HIV and DOA.
I screen your friends, not so much for
good breeding as crack pipes, razor-
cuts and concealed weapons.

Time to wake up, Honey.
Time to tell your Daddy
that everything is going to be OK.
The full moon is smirking at the window.
Tickle-Me-Elmo
is whispering obscenities.
There is something in my closet
that looks like Britney, Beyonce or Christina,
someone I wanted to meet
before I met you.

Big Night

"To eat beautiful food
Is to know God"

No doubt about it, I think,
as I add a bit of garlic and hold off on
the basil until the very last moment,
there is something way sensual here.

All the oni's and ini's, oro's and iti's,
linguini luxuriating on the plate,
the rich red pomodoro sauce palimpsest with spice.
No doubt about it, these people
can really cook.

Culingioni, my Mu-zarella, I propose, knowing
that no woman's honor can withstand my
Penne, al dente, di Vitello.
Pecorino, you smirk at me, Chianti,
Brunello, Rosso,
Barolo,

Focaccio, I threaten, Bracioli Ripieni di Rape,
Fegato, you accuse playfully, Stufato di Manzo
Funghi, I snarl back, but of course

soon everything will be Gnocchi,
we'll Zampone as the bed squeaks
and the neighbors wonder
at the shouting:

Osso Bucco!
Mascarpone!
Pasta!
Pasta!
Pasta!

Delta Connection

- DL 1891, Chicago to Atlanta

Although we have been painstakingly screened
profiled and judged safe in our flat, non-
threatening pan-Anglican features
by the cheerful government-paid airport staff
in their ill-fitting paramilitary uniforms;

although we have herded ourselves in,
strapped ourselves down,
mouthed the familiar mantra
of FAA-mandated safety precautions,
and accepted our duties as exit row wardens,
yet our fingers

foment social revolution.
They intertwine beneath the armrest and slide outside
the pre-assigned boundaries of 27D and 27E,
inflamed with the memory of last night's campaign,
beyond all allegiance,
all restraint, all inhibition.

They are committed to the Cause, these bold digits
that remember earlier irreverence, they who have
torn the tags off mattresses,
raised in solitary salute to fellow drivers,
pointed out the flaws in professors' logic
and so lately traversed the landscapes of our bodies.

Now, empowered, inspired,
they tease the Ché of the imagination
as another hand reaches for a blanket
and two pair of insurrectionist eyes
dance in triumph at 10,000 feet,
and climbing.

Patriotica

When we love we are like
all the people coming together to make
America.

We are Manifest Destiny,
the great exploration, boldly going where
no white one went before,
Lewis and Clark,
Sacagawea, Pocahontas,
Geronimo! Wagons Ho!
Walt Whitman, Horace Greeley,
Opening of the West! Go, Young Man!

And when we love we are like every battle hymn
of our Republic, drunk with our freedom.
Jingoists, super-national patriots, I won't go down
with the ship that has not yet begun to fight,
I won't fire until I see the whites of your eyes;
we are the majesty of the purple mountains,
the waving amber grains oh say, see
and trip the light fantastic I sing America.

Oh, when we love we are like
all the people coming together to make
America. I am Superman and
Paul Bunyan, you are surely
Wonder Woman and Ms. Liberty.
We lay our hands across the sea, make
one nation under God and indivisible,
your Presbyterian and my Jew melding together
in that Great Molten American Pot
conceived and dedicated
of, by and for the people
from sea to shining sea
and truly America the Beautiful.

I Stop to Ponder the Stentorian Colors of the Day

The railing down from the deck
to the garbage cans was wobbly
so I bought a box saw, found an old
two-by-four and some three penny nails
(I think that's what they're called) and
got to work.

A dog was barking, yelling his name
at the dog next door
Big Dog Who Swims! Big Dog Who Swims!
To which his neighbor barked back,
Dog Who Hates Cats! and
some nearby mutt yapped
Mama's Favorite! Mama's Favorite!

A cardinal was shouting *Beauty!*
A mockingbird said
the same, of course.

A chameleon shot out of the hedge,
stopped by my foot, and turning from green
to almost-brown, sneered
You can't see me!, then skittered off.

The sky was whispering until
I looked up and it screamed
Forever!
to which the grass responded
Joy is fragile!

And the saw
sang in my hands
and the wood?
Come on, now. An old two-by-four
with a bent nail in its heart?
Everyone knows dead wood
has nothing to say.

Contributors

Jerri Beck works at a Birmingham bookstore and vounteers as a docent at the Birmingham Zoo. Many of her poems draw on the lessons of words, actions, and good intentions she learned growing up on the Cherokee reservation. The combination of unique experiences and bipolar disorder leads her to ask questions, some of which lead to poems rather than answers.

Robert Boliek practices law in Birmingham, Alabama. Many of his poems are meditations on the worlds of nature and science, of history, and of art. He hopes they challenge the notion that the humanities and the sciences constitute opposite poles of insight and experience by embracing instead what he believes is a common culture of curiosity and wonder.

Suzanne Coker is a veteran performance and page poet. Currently in training to become a radiology technician, she lives in Helena, Alabama, and scratches out poems on whatever scraps of paper she can find. Her motive for writing is best described by Terry Tempest Williams: "I write because then I do not have to speak."

Irene Latham writes to explore the complexity of human relationships, particularly in terms of love, loss, and longing. Married with three sons, she says poetry is her passion and her escape.

Barry Marks says that his poetry is the result of his attempts to make connections with and between the people, places and objects around him. When he is not writing poetry he practices law.